FOR ALLAH
THE LORD AND CREATOR OF THE UNIVERSE

Light on the Tongue

© N. J. Islam & R. D. Verma 1434 AH/ 2013 CE

First Published: July 2013

Published by: ScatteredMoths, PO Box 1147,
                                     Harrow, HA1 9LD, United Kingdom

Compiled by: N. J. Islam

Translation and trans-
literation of 'The Words',
and typesetting by: Abdassamad Clarke

General Editor: Razaan D. Verma

Researchers: Inaam A. Samarasingher
                                     Zaahirah R. Esmail

Cover Design: Cypher Design
                                     www.cyphergraphics.com

Printed and Bound in
Istanbul, Turkey by: Mega Printing
                                     www.mega.com.tr/en

Website: www.scatteredmoths.com

E-mail: info@scatteredmoths.com

A catalogue record of this book is available from the British
Library.

ISBN-13:   978-0-9576537-0-2

LIGHT ON THE TONGUE

COMPILED BY N. J. ISLAM
EDITED BY R. D. VERMA

SCATTEREDMOTHS®

LONDON 2013

CONTENTS

TABLE OF TRANSLITERATION

ء	'	ر	r
ا	a	ز	z
ب	b	س	s
ت	t	ش	sh
ث	th	ص	ṣ
ج	j	ض	ḍ
ح	ḥ	ط	ṭ
خ	kh	ظ	ẓ
د	d	ع	'
ذ	dh	غ	gh

x

ف	f	SHORT VOWEL
ق	q	َ a [*fatḥah*]
ك	k	ُ u [*ḍammah*]
ل	l	ِ i [*kasrah*]
م	m	
ن	n	LONG VOWEL
ه	h	ا ā
و	w	و ū
ي	y	ي ī

ACKNOWLEDGEMENTS

THERE IS no deity worthy of worship but Allāh ﷻ. All praise and gratitude are due to Allāh ﷻ, the Lord of the Worlds and the Creator of all that exists. O Allāh! Bestow Your blessings and peace upon our beloved Prophet Muḥammad ﷺ, his family and his companions, and bless him and his household in the same way as You have blessed Ibrāhīm ﷺ and his household. You are indeed worthy of all Praise, full of Glory.

O Allāh! Please accept and reward the efforts of those who have helped (directly and indirectly) to compile this humble book, and please forgive us for any mistakes we have inadvertently made within these pages.

Āmīn

NARRATED 'AISHAH: The Prophet was asked, "What deeds are loved most by Allah?" He said, "The most regular constant deeds even though they may be few."

[*Sahih al-Bukhari*, Vol. 8, Book of *ar-Riqaq* (Softening of the Hearts), Chapter 18, Hadith No. 6465]

INTRODUCTION

THE PERFORMANCE of obligatory 'Worldly' and 'After-Worldly' duties leaves many Muslims with very little time to do much else. Responsibilities such as studying, performing the five pillars of Islam, engaging in *da'wah*, family commitments, and working full-time compels some to understandably question whether doing 'much else' is even possible. Yet there is a deep yearning in the hearts of many Muslims to do just a little bit more, especially when an opportunity presents itself. There is an earnest hope that additional acts of worship will help to compensate for at least some of the shortcomings that are incurred during one's life.

Light on the Tongue is a small book with a very simple purpose – quick rewards

إِنْ شَاءَ اللَّه. The miserable condition of the Muslim world today is a strong indication of where more effort needs to be expended. Consequently, this little book can be viewed as a 'vitamin pill' to be taken as a supplement for one's spiritual well-being, but it should never become a substitute for nourishing 'foods and drinks' – in other words, our *farḍ* obligations.

May our Lord and Creator, Allāh ﷻ revitalise our minds, bodies and souls so that we may better ourselves and become capable of improving the plight of the Ummah. May He forgive the sins that we undoubtedly incur (knowingly and unknowingly) throughout our lives, and grant us the unfathomable blessing of Jannah.

Āmīn

N. J. Islam

24/7

THE REWARDS

RECITE BEAUTIFUL words that are light on the tongue but heavy on the Scales! Recite two short phrases loved by our Most Merciful Creator, Allāh ﷻ. اِنْ شَاءَ اللَّهُ تَعَالَى.

THE EVIDENCE

Narrated Abu Hurairah ﷺ: The Prophet ﷺ said,

"(There are) two expressions (sayings) which are dear to the Most Gracious (Allah) and very easy for the tongue to say, but very heavy in weight in the balance. They are: '*Subhan Allahi wa bihamdihi*' and '*Subhan Allahil–'Azim*'."

[*Sahih al-Bukhari*, Vol. 9, The Book of *Tauhid*, Chapter 58, Hadith No. 7563]

3

THE WORDS

سُبْحَانَ اللَّهِ وَبِحَمْدِهِ سُبْحَانَ اللَّهِ الْعَظِيمِ

*Subḥān-Allāhi wa bi ḥamdihi subḥān-
Allāhi-l-ʿaẓīm*

Glorious is Allāh and with His Praise,
Glorious is Allāh the Tremendous

Remember: Some foods taste light and yummy on the tongue but end up with you being heavier on the scales! These beautiful words add weight where you need it the most – on the right side of the Scales on Judgement Day إِنْ شَاءَ اللَّه.

THE REWARDS

CANCEL OUT your sins even if they are like the foam of the sea. Recite words that are the *most* loved by Allāh ﷻ إِنْ شَاءَ اللَّهُ.

THE EVIDENCE

Narrated Abu Hurairah ؓ: Allah's Messenger ﷺ said:

"Whoever says, '*Subhan Allahi wa bihamdihi,*' one hundred times a day, will be forgiven all his sins even if they were as much as the foam of the sea."

[*Sahih al-Bukhari*, Vol. 8, The Book of Invocations, Chapter 65, Hadith No. 6405]

It was narrated that Abu Dharr ؓ said: "The Messenger of Allah ﷺ said: 'Shall I not tell you of the dearest of words to Allah?' I said: 'Yes, O Messenger of Allah, tell me which words are dearest to Allah.' He said: 'The dearest of words to Allah are: *Subhan Allahi wa bi-hamdih* (Glory to Allah and with His praise).'"

[*Sahih Muslim*, Vol. 7, Remembrance, Supplication, Repentance and Praying for Forgiveness, Chapter 22, Hadith No. (6926) 85 – (...)]

The Words

Subhān-Allāhi wa bi ḥamdih

Glorious is Allāh and with His Praise

Remember: Recite this phrase 100 times a day and have loads of sins wiped away; and should you fail to meet this score, you have still recited what Your Lord adores!

THE REWARDS

RECEIVE 1000 good deeds. Erase 1000 bad deeds إِنْ شَاءَ اللَّهُ.

THE EVIDENCE

It was narrated from Mus'ab bin Sa'd: My father ﷺ told me: "We were with the Messenger of Allah ﷺ and he said: 'Is it too difficult for any one of you to earn one thousand *Hasanah* (good deeds) every day?' One of those who were sitting with him asked him: 'How can one of us earn one thousand *Hasanah*?' He said: 'If he says one hundred *Tasbih*, (saying 'Subhan Allah) then one thousand *Hasanah* will be recorded for him, and one thousand bad deeds will be erased for him.'"

[*Sahih Muslim*, Vol. 7, Remembrance, Supplication, Repentance and Praying for Forgiveness, Chapter 10, Hadith No. (6852) 37 – (2698)]

THE WORDS

سُبْحَانَ اللَّهِ (١٠٠)

Subḥān-Allāh (x100)

Glorious is Allāh (x100)

Remember: Swap fruitless words of hate and get your mind into an Islamic state. *Subḥān-Allāh* – a tiny phrase that packs a mighty punch! We can increase our rewards by counting '*Subḥān-Allāh*' on our right hand thus simultaneously performing a *Sunnah* deed too.

'Abdullah bin 'Amr ﷺ narrated: "I saw the Messenger of Allah ﷺ count the *Tasbih*." Ibn Qudamah (one of the narrators) added: "With his right hand."

[*Sunan Abu Dawud*, Vol. 2, The Book of *Witr*, Chapter 24, Hadith No. 1502]

THE REWARD

HAVE A date-palm tree planted for you in Paradise إِنْ شَاءَ اللَّهُ.

THE EVIDENCE

Jabir ⬧ narrated that the Prophet ⬧ said: "Whoever says: 'Glory is to Allah, the Magnificent, and with His Praise (*Subhan Allahil-'Azim, Wa Bihamdih*)' a date-palm tree is planted for him in Paradise."

[*Jami' at-Tirmidhi*, Vol. 6, The Book of Supplications, Chapter 59, Hadith No. 3464]

THE WORDS

سُبْحَانَ اللَّهِ الْعَظِيمِ وَبِحَمْدِهِ

Subḥān-Allāhi-l-'Aẓīmi wa biḥamdih

Glorious is Allāh the Magnificent, and with His Praise

Remember: Abu Hurairah ﷺ narrated that the Messenger of Allah ﷺ said: "There is not a tree in Paradise except that its trunk is of gold."

[*Jami' at-Tirmidhi*, Vol. 4, The Description of Paradise, Chapter 1, Hadith No. 2525]

THE REWARDS

RECITE ONE-THIRD of the Qur'ān in minutes. Make *Jannah* obligatory for you. Wipe out the sins of 50 years إِنْ شَاءَ اللَّهُ.

THE EVIDENCE

It was narrated from Abu Ad-Darda' ؓ that the Prophet ﷺ said: "Is any one of you incapable of reciting one-third of the Qur'an during the night?" They said: "How could he recite one-third of the Qur'an?" He said: "Say: "He is Allah the One" is equivalent to one-third of the Qur'an."

[*Sahih Muslim*, Vol. 2, The Book of the Virtues of the Qur'an etc., Chapter 45, Hadith No. (1886) 259 – (811)]

Abu Hurairah ﷺ said: "I went out with the Messenger of Allah and heard a man reciting *Qul Huwa Allahu Ahad* (*Allahus-Samad*) so the Messenger of Allah ﷺ said: 'It is obligatory.' I said: 'What is obligatory?' He said: 'Paradise.'"

[*Jami' at-Tirmidhi*, Vol. 5, The Virtues of the Qur'an, Chapter 11, Hadith No. 2897]

Anas bin Malik ﷺ narrated that The Prophet ﷺ said:

"Whoever recited *Qul Huwa Allahu Ahad* two hundred times every day, fifty years worth of his sins will be removed – unless he owes a debt."

[*Jami' at-Tirmidhi*, Vol. 5, The Virtues of the Qur'an, Chapter 11, Hadith No. 2898]

THE WORDS

سورة الإخلاص

قُلْ هُوَ ٱللَّهُ أَحَدٌ

ٱللَّهُ ٱلصَّمَدُ لَمْ يَلِدْ وَلَمْ يُولَدْ

وَلَمْ يَكُنْ لَّهُ كُفُوًا أَحَدٌ

Sūrah al-Ikhlāṣ
Qul huwa-llāhu aḥad
Allāhu-ṣ-ṣamad
Lam yalid wa lam yūlad
Wa lam yaku-l-lahu kufuwan aḥad

Say: 'He is Allāh, Absolute Oneness,
Allāh, the Everlasting Sustainer of all.
He has not given birth and was not
born.
And no one is comparable to Him.'

Remember: *Sūrah al-Ikhlāṣ* is an excellent way to gain lots of rewards in a short period of time. Nonetheless, we should not consider this as a replacement for the actual study and recitation of the Noble Qur'ān, which consists of the literal Words of Allāh and is the living 'Miracle of Islam'.

THE REWARD

REPLACE CALAMITIES with something better .اِنْ شَاءَ اللَّهُ

THE EVIDENCE

It was narrated that Umm Salamah ؓ said: "I heard the Messenger of Allah ﷺ say:

'There is no Muslim who is stricken with a calamity and says what Allah has enjoined – *Innalillahi wainna ilaihi raji'un. Allahummajurni fi musibati wa akhlif li khairan minha* (Verily to Allah we belong and unto Him is our return. O Allah, reward me for my affliction and compensate me with something better) – but Allah will compensate him with something better.'"

[*Sahih Muslim*, Vol. 2, Book of Funerals, Chapter 2, Hadith No. (2126), 3 – (918)]

THE WORDS

إِنَّا لِلَّهِ وَإِنَّا إِلَيْهِ رَاجِعُونَ . اَللَّهُمَّ أَجِرْنِي فِي مُصِيبَتِي، وَأَخْلِفْ لِي خَيْراً مِّنْها

Innā lillāhi wa innā ilayhi rāji'ūn.
Allāhumma ajirnī fī muṣībatī wa akhlif lī khayram-minhā

To Allāh we belong, and to Him we return. O Allah reward me for my calamity and give me something better than it.

Remember: Our Lord! Impose not on us that which we have not the strength to bear. Grant us Your forgiveness and shower Your bountiful Mercy upon us. Should a calamity occur, pour out on us patience, wisdom and the strength to bear it in a manner that pleases You. Allow us to remember this *du'ā* so that we may comfort ourselves and others with the remembrance that You, O Merciful One will give us something better than that we have lost. Verily, You never fail to fulfil Your promise. *Āmīn.*

THE REWARDS

GET 100 good deeds recorded for you. Wipe away 100 bad deeds. Gain refuge from the devil until evening. Earn rewards equivalent to freeing 4 slaves from the Children of Isma'il. And more! اِنْ شَاءَ اللَّهُ.

THE EVIDENCE

It was narrated from Abu Hurairah ﷺ that the Messenger of Allah ﷺ said: "Whoever says: '*La ilaha illallahu wahdahu la sharika lahu, lahulmulku wa lahul-hamdu, wa huwa 'ala kulli shay'in qadir* (None has the right to be worshipped but Allah alone with no partner or associate, His is the dominion, to Him is praise and He has power over all things)' one hundred times in a day, it will be the equivalent of his freeing one hundred slaves, and one hundred good deeds will be recorded for him, and one hundred bad deeds will be erased for him, and it will be a protection for him against the *Shaitan* all day until evening comes, and no one will do anything better than what he has done except one who does more than that."

[*Sahih Muslim*, Vol. 7, Remembrance, Supplication, Repentance and Praying for Forgiveness, Chapter 10, Hadith No. (6842) 28 – (2691)]

It was narrated that 'Amr bin Maimun said:

"Whoever says: '*La ilaha illallahu wahdahu la sharika lahu, lahul-mulku wa lahul-hamdu, wa huwa 'ala kulli shay'in qadir* (None has the right to be worshipped but Allah alone with no partner or associate, His is the dominion, to Him be praise and He has power over all things)' ten times, he will be like one who freed four slaves among the sons of Isma'il."

[*Sahih Muslim*, Vol. 7, Remembrance, Supplication, Repentance and Praying for Forgiveness, Chapter 10, Hadith No. (6844) 30 – (2693)]

A similar report (as *Hadith* no. 6844) was narrated from Ash-Sha'bi from Rabi' bin Khuthaim. (Ash-Sha'bi) said: "I said to Rabi': 'From whom did you hear it?' He said: 'From 'Amr bin Maimun.'" He said: "I went to 'Amr bin Maimun and said: 'From whom did you hear it?' He said: 'From Ibn Abi Laila.'" He said: "I went to Ibn Abi Laila and said: 'From whom did you hear it?' He said: 'From Abu Ayyub Al-Ansari ﷺ, who narrated it from the Messenger of Allah ﷺ.'"

[*Sahih Muslim*, Vol. 7, Remembrance, Supplication, Repentance and Praying for Forgiveness, Chapter 10, Hadith No. (6845) (...)]

THE WORDS

لَاۤ إِلَهَ إِلَّا اللَّهُ وَحْدَهُ لَا شَرِيكَ لَهُ،

لَهُ الْمُلْكُ وَلَهُ الْحَمْدُ،

وَهُوَ عَلَى كُلِّ شَيْءٍ قَدِيرٌ

Lā ilāha illa-llāhu waḥdahu lā sharīka lah,
lahu-l-mulku wa lahu-l-ḥamd,
wa Huwa ʿalā kulli shay'in qadīr

There is no god but Allāh alone Who
has no partner. His is the kingdom and
His is the praise, and He is able to do all
things.

Remember: *Shirk* (association of partners
with Allāh ﷻ) is an unforgivable crime.
All other sins have the potential to be
forgiven by Allāh ﷻ but not *shirk*! This
duʿā not only allows us the opportunity
to gain lots of rewards but it lets us
wholeheartedly confirm that our Lord
and Creator Allāh ﷻ is the One and Only
God.

THE REWARD

RECITE THESE four beautiful phrases for lots of rewards إِنْ شَاءَ اللَّهُ.

THE EVIDENCE

It was narrated from Juwayriyah ﷺ that the Prophet ﷺ left her one morning when he prayed *Subh*, (i.e. *Fajr* prayer) and she was in her prayer-place, then he came back after the forenoon had come, and she was still sitting there. He said: "Are you still as you were when I left you?" She said: "Yes." The Prophet ﷺ said: "After I left you I said four words three times, which if they were weighed against what you have said today, they would outweigh it: *Subhan-Allahi wa bi-hamdihi 'adada khalqihi, wa rida nafsihi, wa zinata 'arshihi, wa midada kalimatih*

(Glory and praise is to Allāh, as much as the number of His creation, as much as pleases Him, as much as the weight of His Throne and as much as the ink of His words)."

[*Sahih Muslim*, Vol. 7, Remembrance, Supplication, Repentance and Praying for Forgiveness, Chapter 19, Hadith No. (6913) 79 – (2726)]

THE WORDS

سُبْحَانَ اللَّهِ وَبِحَمْدِهِ

عَدَدَ خَلْقِهِ

وَرَضَاءَ نَفْسِهِ

وَزِنَةَ عَرْشِهِ وَمِدَادَ كَلِمَاتِهِ

*Subḥān-Allāhi wa bi ḥamdihi,
'adada khalqihi,
wa riḍā'a nafsihi,*

wa zinata 'arshihi,
wa midāda kalimātih

Glorious is Allāh and with His Praise
according to the number of His creation,
and as much as His Pleasure,
and as much as the weight of His Throne
and the ink of His Words

Remember: *And if all the trees on*
earth were pens and the Ocean (were ink),
with seven Oceans behind it to add to its
(supply), yet would not the Words of Allāh
be exhausted (in the writing): for Allāh is
Exalted in Power, Full of Wisdom.

[Holy Qur'ān, Sūrah Luqmān 31:27]

THE REWARD

GET FORTY million good deeds recorded for you إِنْ شَاءَ اللَّهُ.

THE EVIDENCE

Tamim Ad-Dari ﷺ narrated that the Messenger of Allah ﷺ said: "Whoever says ten times: 'I bear witness that none has the right to be worshipped but Allah. Alone, without partner, One Deity, the One, *As-Samad*, He did not take a wife, nor a child, nor is there anyone like Him, (*Ashhadu An La Ilaha Illallah, Wahdahu La Sharika Lahu, Ilahan Wahidan, Ahadan Samadan Lam Yattakhidh Sahibatan Wa La Waladan Wa Lam Yakun Lahu Kufuwan Ahad)*' Allah will write for him forty million good deeds."

[*Jami' at-Tirmidhi*, Vol. 6, The Book of Supplications, Chapter 62, Hadith No. 3473]

THE WORDS

أَشْهَدُ أَنْ لَا آإِلَهَ إِلَّا اللَّهُ وَحْدَهُ لَا شَرِيكَ
لَهُ، إِلَهاً وَاحِداً، أَحَداً، صَمَداً،
لَمْ يَتَّخِذْ صَاحِبَةً وَلاَ وَلَداً،
وَلَمْ يَكُنْ لَّهُ كُفُواً أَحَدٌ.

Ash-hadu al-lā ilāha illa-llāhu waḥdahu
lā sharīka lah, Ilāhan Wāḥidan, Aḥadan,
Ṣamadan, lam yattakhidh ṣāḥibatan wa
la waladan, wa lam yaku-l-lahu kufuwan
Aḥad

I bear witness that none has the right
to be worshipped but Allāh alone,
without partner, One, Single, aṣ-Ṣamad,
He did not take a wife, nor a child, nor
is there anyone like Him

Remember: *And behold! Allāh will say: "O Jesus the son of Mary! Didst thou say unto men, 'Worship me and my mother as gods in derogation of Allāh'?" He will say: "Glory to Thee! Never could I say what I had no right (to say). Had I said such a thing, Thou wouldst indeed have known it. Thou knowest what is in my heart, though I know not what is in Thine. For Thou knowest in full all that is hidden."*

[Holy Qur'ān, Sūrat al-Mā'idah 5:116]

THE REWARD

KEEP THE *shayṭān* away from you!
.إِنْ شَاءَ اللَّهُ

THE EVIDENCE

'Abdur-Rahman bin Abi Laila narrated that Abu Ayyub Al-Ansari ﷺ had a store house in which he kept dates. A ghoul would come and take from it, so he complained about that to the Prophet ﷺ. So he said: "Go, and when you see her say: 'In the Name of Allah, answer to the Messenger of Allah ﷺ.'" He said: "So I caught her, and she swore that she would not return, so I released her." He went to the Prophet ﷺ and he said: "What did your captive do?" He said: "She swore not to return." He said: "She has lied, and she will come again to lie."

He said: "I caught her another time and she swore that she would not return, so I released her, and went to the Prophet ﷺ." He said: "What did your captive do?" He said: "She swore that she would not return." So he said: "She lied and she will come again to lie." So he caught her and said: "I shall not let you go until you accompany me to the Prophet ﷺ." She said: "I shall tell you something: If you recite *Ayat Al-Kursi* in your home, then no *Shaitan*, nor any other shall come near you." So he went to the Prophet ﷺ and he said: "What did your captive do?" He said: "I informed him of what she said, and he said: 'She told the truth and she is a continuous liar.'"

[*Jami' at-Tirmidhi*, Vol. 5, The Virtues of the Qur'an, Chapter 3, Hadith No. 2880]

THE WORDS

آيَةُ الكرسي

بِسْمِ ٱللَّهِ ٱلرَّحْمَٰنِ ٱلرَّحِيمِ

ٱللَّهُ لَآ إِلَٰهَ إِلَّا هُوَ ٱلْحَىُّ ٱلْقَيُّومُ ۚ

لَا تَأْخُذُهُۥ سِنَةٌ وَلَا نَوْمٌ ۚ

لَّهُۥ مَا فِى ٱلسَّمَٰوَٰتِ وَمَا فِى ٱلْأَرْضِ ۗ

مَن ذَا ٱلَّذِى يَشْفَعُ عِندَهُۥٓ إِلَّا بِإِذْنِهِۦ ۚ

يَعْلَمُ مَا بَيْنَ أَيْدِيهِمْ وَمَا خَلْفَهُمْ ۖ

وَلَا يُحِيطُونَ بِشَىْءٍ مِّنْ عِلْمِهِۦٓ إِلَّا بِمَا شَآءَ ۚ

وَسِعَ كُرْسِيُّهُ ٱلسَّمَٰوَٰتِ وَٱلْأَرْضَ ۖ

وَلَا يَؤُودُهُ حِفْظُهُمَا ۚ وَهُوَ الْعَلِيُّ الْعَظِيمُ

Bismillāhi-r-Raḥmāni-r-Raḥīm
Allāhu lā ilāha illā Hū, al-Ḥayyu-l-Qayyūm
Lā ta'khudhuhū sinatun wa lā nawm,
lahū mā fi-s-samāwāti wa mā fi-l-arḍ
Man dha-l-ladhī yashfa'u 'indahu
illā bi-idhnihi
Ya'lamu mā bayna aydīhim
wa mā khalfahum,
wa lā yuḥīṭūna bi shay'im-min
'ilmihī illā bimā shā'a
Wasi'a kursiyyuhu-s-samāwāti wa-l-arḍ,
wa la ya'ūduhu ḥifẓuhumā, Wa Huwa-l-
'Aliyyu-l-'Aẓīm

In the name of Allāh,
All-Merciful, Most Merciful
Allāh, there is no god but Him, the
Living, the Self-Sustaining. He is
not subject to drowsiness or sleep.
Everything in the heavens and the

earth belongs to Him. Who can intercede with Him except by His permission? He knows what is before them and what is behind them but they cannot grasp any of His knowledge save what He wills. His Footstool encompasses the heavens and the earth and their preservation does not tire Him. He is the Most High, the Magnificent.

Remember: It was narrated that Anas bin Malik ﷺ said: "The Messenger of Allah ﷺ said: 'The *Shaitan* flows through the son of Adam like blood.'"

[*Sunan Abu Dawud*, Vol. 5, The Book of the *Sunnah*, Chapter 17, Hadith No. 4719]

THE REWARD

MEMORISE THE 99 beautiful Names of Allāh ﷻ and gain entry into Paradise إِنْ شَاءَ اللّٰهُ.

THE EVIDENCE

Narrated Abu Hurairah ﷺ: Allah's Messenger ﷺ said,

"Allah has ninety-nine Names, one-hundred less one; and he who memorised them all by heart will enter Paradise."

[*Sahih al-Bukhari*, Vol. 9, Book of *Tauhid*, Chapter 12, Hadith No. 7392]

THE WORDS

بِسْمِ اللّٰهِ الرَّحْمٰنِ الرَّحِيْمُ

	Arabic	Transliteration	Translation
1	الرَّحْمَٰنِ	Ar-Raḥmān	The All Merciful
2	الرَّحِيمِ	Ar-Raḥīm	The Most Merciful
3	الْمَلِكُ	Al-Malik	The King
4	الْقُدُّوسُ	Al-Quddūs	The Most Holy, the Most Pure
5	السَّلَامُ	As-Salām	The Source of Peace
6	الْمُؤْمِنُ	Al-Mu'min	The Granter of Security
7	الْمُهَيْمِنُ	Al-Muhaymin	The Guardian
8	الْعَزِيزُ	Al-'Azīz	The Almighty
9	الْجَبَّارُ	Al-Jabbār	The Compeller
10	الْمُتَكَبِّرُ	Al-Mutakabbir	The Tremendous
11	الْخَالِقُ	Al-Khāliq	The Creator
12	الْبَارِئُ	Al-Bāri'	The Maker

13	الْمُصَوِّرُ	Al-Muṣawwir	The Giver of Form
14	الْغَفَّارُ	Al-Ghaffār	The Ever Forgiving
15	الْقَهَّارُ	Al-Qahhār	The All Compelling Subduer
16	الْوَهَّابُ	Al-Wahhāb	The Ever Bestowing
17	الرَّزَّاقُ	Ar-Razzāq	The Ever Providing
18	الْفَتَّاحُ	Al-Fattāḥ	The Opener
19	الْعَلِيمُ	Al-ʿAlīm	The All Knowing
20	الْقَابِضُ	Al-Qābiḍ	The Restrainer
21	الْبَاسِطُ	Al-Bāsiṭ	The Expander
22	الْخَافِضُ	Al-Khāfiḍ	The Abaser
23	الرَّافِعُ	Ar-Rāfiʿ	The Exalter
24	الْمُعِزُّ	Al-Muʿizz	The Giver of Honour
25	الْمُذِلُّ	Al-Mudhill	The Humbler

26	السَّمِيعُ	As-Samī'	The All Hearing
27	الْبَصِيرُ	Al-Baṣīr	The All Seeing
28	الْحَكَمُ	Al-Ḥakam	The Judge
29	الْعَدْلُ	Al-'Adl	The Utterly Just
30	اللَّطِيفُ	Al-Laṭīf	The Gentle
31	الْخَبِيرُ	Al-Khabīr	The All Aware
32	الْحَلِيمُ	Al-Ḥalīm	The Forbearing
33	الْعَظِيمُ	Al-'Aẓīm	The Magnificent
34	الْغَفُورُ	Al-Ghafūr	The All Forgiving
35	الشَّكُورُ	Ash-Shakūr	The Grateful
36	الْعَلِيُّ	Al-'Alī	The Sublimely Exalted
37	الْكَبِيرُ	Al-Kabīr	The Great
38	الْحَفِيظُ	Al-Ḥafīẓ	The Preserver

39	الْمُقِيت	Al-Muqīt	The Nourisher
40	الْحَسِيب	Al-Ḥasīb	The Reckoner
41	الْجَلِيل	Al-Jalīl	The Majestic
42	الْكَرِيم	Al-Karīm	The Generously Noble
43	الرَّقِيب	Ar-Raqīb	The Vigilant
44	الْمُجِيب	Al-Mujīb	The Answerer
45	الْوَاسِع	Al-Wāsiʿ	The Vast
46	الْحَكِيم	Al-Ḥakīm	The Wise
47	الْوَدُود	Al-Wadūd	The One Who Loves
48	الْمَجِيد	Al-Majīd	The All Glorious
49	الْبَاعِث	Al-Bāʿith	The Raiser of The Dead
50	الشَّهِيد	Ash-Shahīd	The Witness
51	الْحَقّ	Al-Ḥaqq	The Truth

52	الْوَكِيلُ	Al-Wakīl	The Trustee
53	الْقَوِىُّ	Al-Qawī	The Strong
54	الْمَتِينُ	Al-Matīn	The Firm
55	الْوَلِىُّ	Al-Walī	The Protecting Friend
56	الْحَمِيدُ	Al-Ḥamīd	The All Praiseworthy
57	الْمُحْصِي	Al-Muḥsī	The One Who Comprehends Everything
58	الْمُبْدِئُ	Al-Mubdi'	The Producer
59	الْمُعِيدُ	Al-Mu'īd	The Restorer
60	الْمُحْيِي	Al-Muḥyī	The Giver of Life
61	الْمُمِيتُ	Al-Mumīt	The Bringer of Death
62	الْحَيُّ	Al-Ḥayy	The Ever Living

63	الْقَيُّوُمُ	Al-Qayyūm	The Self Subsisting Provider
64	الْوَاجِدُ	Al-Wājid	The Perceiver
65	الْمَاجِدُ	Al-Mājid	The Illustrious
66	الْوَاحِدُ	Al-Wāḥid	The One
67	الْأَحَدُ	Al-Aḥad	The Single
68	الصَّمَدُ	Aṣ-Ṣamad	The Self Sufficient
69	الْقَادِرُ	Al-Qādir	The All Able
70	الْمُقْتَدِرُ	Al-Muqtadir	The Dominant
71	الْمُقَدِّمُ	Al-Muqaddim	The Expediter
72	الْمُؤَخِّرُ	Al-Mu'akhkhir	The Delayer
73	الْأَوَّلُ	Al-Awwal	The First
74	الْآخِرُ	Al-Ākhir	The Last
75	الظَّاهِرُ	Aẓ-Ẓāhir	The Outwardly Apparent

76	الْبَاطِنُ	Al-Bāṭin	The Inwardly Hidden
77	الْوَالِي	Al-Wālī	The Patron
78	الْمُتَعَالِي	Al-Mutaʻālī	The Self Exalted
79	الْبَرُّ	Al-Barr	The Wholly Good
80	التَّوَّابُ	At-Tawwāb	The Ever Returning
81	الْمُنْتَقِمُ	Al-Muntaqim	The Avenger
82	الْعَفُوُّ	Al-ʻAfū	The Pardoner
83	الرَّؤُوفُ	Ar-Raʼūf	The Compassionate
84	مَالِكُ الْمُلْكِ	Māliku-l-Mulk	The Owner of All Sovereignty
85	ذُو الْجَلَالِ وَالْإِكْرَامِ	Dhū-l-Jalāli wa-l-Ikrām	The Lord of Majesty and Generosity
86	الْمُقْسِطُ	Al-Muqsiṭ	The Equitable
87	الْجَامِعُ	Al-Jāmiʻ	The Gatherer

88	الْغَنِيُّ	Al-Ghanī	The Free of Need
89	الْمُغْنِي	Al-Mughnī	The One Who Frees from Need
90	الْمَانِعُ	Al-Māni'	The Defender
91	الضَّارُّ	Aḍ-Ḍārr	The Afflicter
92	النَّافِعُ	An-Nāfi'	The Benefactor
93	النُّورُ	An-Nūr	The Light
94	الْهَادِي	Al-Hādī	The Guide
95	الْبَدِيعُ	Al-Badī'	The Incomparable
96	الْبَاقِي	Al-Bāqī	The Ever Enduring
97	الْوَارِثُ	Al-Wārith	The Inheritor
98	الرَّشِيدُ	Ar-Rashīd	The Guide
99	الصَّبُورُ	Aṣ-Ṣabūr	The Patient

Remember: Memorising all the beautiful names of Allāh ﷻ may seem a bit daunting if we attempt to do it all at once (unless you have the memory of an elephant!). We can try and memorise three names a day or even one a day, and thus reach our goal in an undemanding and achievable manner اِنْ شَاءَ اللّٰه.

DUSK TO DAWN

THE REWARDS

HAVE 70,000 angels invoke blessings upon you. Attain the honoured status of a martyr upon death إِنْ شَاءَ اللَّهُ.

THE EVIDENCE

Ma'qil bin Yasar ؓ narrated that the Prophet ﷺ said: "Whoever says three times when he gets up in the morning: *'A'udhu Billahis-Sami' Al-'Alim Min Ash-Shaitanir-Rajim'* and he recites three Ayat from the end of Surat Al-Hashr – Allāh appoints seventy-thousand angels who say Salat upon him until the evening. If he dies on that day, he dies a martyr, and whoever says them when he reaches the evening, he holds the same status."

[*Jami' at-Tirmidhi*, Vol. 5, The Virtues of the Qur'an, Chapter 22, Hadith No. 2922]

The Words

أَعُوذُ بِاللَّهِ السَّمِيعِ الْعَلِيمِ
مِنَ الشَّيْطَانِ الرَّجِيمِ (٣)

هُوَ اللَّهُ الَّذِى لَآ إِلَٰهَ إِلَّا هُوَ ۖ عَٰلِمُ الْغَيْبِ
وَالشَّهَٰدَةِ ۖ هُوَ الرَّحْمَٰنُ الرَّحِيمُ

هُوَ اللَّهُ الَّذِى لَآ إِلَٰهَ إِلَّا هُوَ ۖ الْمَلِكُ الْقُدُّوسُ
السَّلَٰمُ الْمُؤْمِنُ الْمُهَيْمِنُ الْعَزِيزُ الْجَبَّارُ
الْمُتَكَبِّرُ ۚ سُبْحَٰنَ اللَّهِ عَمَّا يُشْرِكُونَ

هُوَ اللَّهُ الْخَٰلِقُ الْبَارِئُ الْمُصَوِّرُ ۖ لَهُ الْأَسْمَآءُ
الْحُسْنَىٰ ۚ يُسَبِّحُ لَهُ مَا فِى السَّمَٰوَٰتِ
وَالْأَرْضِ ۖ وَهُوَ الْعَزِيزُ الْحَكِيمُ

A'ūdu billāhi-s-samī'i-l-'alīmi mina-sh-
shayṭāni-r-rajīm (x3)

Huwa-llāhu-lladhī lā ilāha illā Hū.
'Ālimu-l-ghaybi wa-sh-shahādah.
Huwa-r-Raḥmānu-r-Raḥīm.
Huwa-llāhu-lladhī lā ilāha illā Huwa-l-
Maliku-l-Quddūsu-s-Salāmu-l-Mu'minu-
l-Muhayminu-l-'Azīzu-l-Jabbāru-l-
Mutakabbir.
Subḥān-Allāhi 'ammā yushrikūn.
Huwa-llāhu-l-Khāliqu-l-Bāri'u-Muṣawwir.
Lahu-l-asmā'u-l-ḥusnā.
Yusabbiḥu lahū mā fi-s-samāwāti wa-l-arḍ.
Wa Huwa-l-'Azīzu-l-Ḥakīm.

I seek refuge in Allāh, the All-Hearing,
the All-Knowing, from the accursed
shayṭān (x3)

Allah is He, than Whom there is no
other god - Who knows (all things) both
secret and open; He, Most Gracious,
Most Merciful. Allah is He, than Whom
there is no other god – the Sovereign,

49

the Holy One, the Source of Peace (and Perfection), the Guardian of Faith, the Preserver of Safety, the Exalted in Might, the Irresistible, the Supreme: glory to Allah! (High is He) above the partners they attribute to Him. He is Allah, the Creator, the Evolver, the Bestower of Forms (or Colours). To Him belong the Most Beautiful Names: whatever is in the heavens and on earth, doth declare His Praises and Glory; and He is the Exalted in Might, the Wise.

[Holy Qur'ān, Sūrat al-Hashr 59:22-24]

Remember: It is these phenomenally rewarding *āyāt* that my beloved mother taught me as a child that ultimately became the inspiration for compiling 'Light on the Tongue' ٱلْحَمْدُ لِلَّٰه.

THE REWARD

BE PROTECTED from hellfire
إِنْ شَاءَ اللَّهُ.

THE EVIDENCE

It was narrated from Muhammad bin Shu'aib: "Abu Sa'eed Al-Filastini 'Abdur-Rahman bin Hassan informed me, from Al-Harith bin Muslim; that he informed him, from his father, Muslim bin Al-Harith At-Tamimi ؓ, that the Messenger of Allah ﷺ whispered to him, and said: 'When you finish *Maghrib* prayer, say: *"Allahumma ajirnimin an-nar* (O Allah, protect me from Hell)"* seven times, for if you say that, then you die that night, protection from it will be decreed for you. And when you pray *Subh* (*Fajr*), say that too, then if you

51

die that day, protection from it will be decreed for you.'"

[*Sunan Abu Dawud*, Vol. 5, The Book of Etiquette, Chapter 100, 101, Hadith No. 5079]

THE WORDS

اَللّٰهُمَّ أَجِرْنِي مِنَ النَّارِ (٧)

Allāhumma ajirnī min an-nar (x7)

O Allāh, protect me from Hell (x7)

Remember: *But those whose balance is light, will be those who have lost their souls; in Hell will they abide. The Fire will burn their faces, and they will therein grin, with their lips displaced. "Were not My Signs rehearsed to you, and ye did but treat them as falsehoods?"*

[Holy Qur'ān, Sūrat al-Mu'minūn 23: 103-105]

52

THE REWARD

Have Allāh ﷻ be sufficient for you against all that causes you distress إِنْ شَاءَ اللّٰهُ.

THE EVIDENCE

It was narrated from Umm Ad-Darda' that Abu Ad-Darda' ؓ said: "Whoever says, morning and evening; *'Hasbiya-llaha la ilaha illa huwa, 'alaihi tawakkaltu, wa huwa rabbul-'arshil-'azim* (Allah is sufficient for me, there is none worthy of worship but He, in Him I have put my trust, and He is the Lord of the Mighty Throne)' seven times, Allah will suffice him against all that grieves him, whether he is sincere when saying it, or not."

[*Sunan Abu Dawud*, Vol. 5, The Book of Etiquette Chapter 100, 101, Hadith No. 5081]

THE WORDS

حَسْبِيَ اللَّهُ لَا إِلَهَ إِلَّا هُوَ، عَلَيْهِ تَوَكَّلْتُ، وَهُوَ رَبُّ الْعَرْشِ الْعَظِيمِ (٧)

*Ḥasbiya-llāhu lā ilāha illā Huwa,
'alayhi tawakkaltu,
wa Huwa Rabbul-'arshil-'aẓīm (x7)*

Allāh is enough for me. There is no god but Him. I have put my trust in Him. He is the Lord of the Mighty Throne. (x7)

Remember: It was narrated from Abu Hurairah ﷺ that the Prophet ﷺ said: "When Allāh created the creation, He wrote in His Book, which is with Him above the Throne: 'My Mercy prevails over My Wrath.'"

[*Sahih Muslim*, Vol. 7, The Book of Repentance, Chapter 4, Hadith No. (6969) 14 – (2751)]

THE REWARD

COMPETE TO bring something great with you on the Day of Resurrection إِنْ شَاءَ اللَّهُ.

THE EVIDENCE

It was narrated from Abu Hurairah ؓ that the Messenger of Allah ﷺ said: "Whoever says in the morning and in the evening: '*Subhan Allahi wa bihamdihi* (Glory and praise is to Allah)' one hundred times, no one will come on the Day of Resurrection with anything better than what he has done, except one who said something like what he said, or more than that."

[*Sahih Muslim*, Vol. 7, Remembrance, Supplication, Repentance and Praying for Forgiveness, Chapter 10, Hadith No. (6843) 29 – (2692)]

THE WORDS

سُبْحَانَ اللَّهِ وَبِحَمْدِهِ (١٠٠)

Subḥān-Allāhi wa bi ḥamdih (x100)

Glorious is Allāh and with His Praise (x100)

Remember: *To each is a goal to which Allah turns him; then strive together (as in a race) towards all that is good. Wheresoever ye are, Allah will bring you together. For Allah hath power over all things.*

[Holy Qur'ān, Sūrat al-Baqarah 2:148]

THE REWARD

B E FROM the people of Paradise
إِنْ شَاءَ اللَّهُ.

THE EVIDENCE

Narrated Shaddad bin Aus 🙐: The
Prophet 🙲 said,

"The most superior way of asking for
forgiveness from Allah is: '*Allahumma
Anta Rabbi la ilaha illa Anta khalaqtani wa
ana 'abduka, wa ana 'ala 'ahdika wa wa'dika
mastata'tu. A'udhu bika min sharri ma
sana'tu, abu'u laka bini'matika 'alaiya, wa
abu'u bidhanbi faghfirli innahu la yaghfirudh-
dhunuba illa Anta.*'" The Prophet 🙲 added,
"If somebody recites it during the day
with firm faith in it, and dies on the same
day before the evening, he will be from
the people of Paradise; and if somebody

recites it at night with firm faith in it, and dies before the morning, he will be from the people of Paradise."

[*Sahih al-Bukhari*, Vol. 8, The Book of Invocations, Chapter 2, Hadith No. 6306]

THE WORDS

اللَّهُمَّ أَنْتَ رَبِّي لَآ إِلَهَ إِلَّا أَنْتَ

خَلَقْتَنِي وَأَنَا عَبْدُكَ وَأَنَا عَلَى عَهْدِكَ وَوَعْدِكَ مَا اسْتَطَعْتُ

أَعُوذُ بِكَ مِنْ شَرِّ مَا صَنَعْتُ

أَبُوءُ لَكَ بِنِعْمَتِكَ عَلَيَّ وَأَبُوءُ لَكَ بِذَنْبِي

فَاغْفِرْ لِي فَإِنَّهُ لَايَغْفِرُ الذُّنُوبَ إِلَّا أَنْتَ

Allāhumma anta Rabbī lā ilāha illā anta,
khalaqtanī wa ana ʿabduka,
wa ana ʿalā ʿahdika wa waʿdika ma-staṭaʿtu,
aʿūdhu bika min sharri mā ṣanaʿtu,
abūʾu laka bi niʿmatika ʿalayya,
wa abūʾu laka bi dhanbī
fa-ghfirlī fa innahu lā yaghfiru-dh-dhunūba
illā anta

Allāh! You are my Lord!
There is no god but You.
You created me and I am Your slave,
and I am faithful to Your covenant
and Your promise as much as I can.
I seek refuge with You from the evil I
have done.
I acknowledge to You the blessings You
have bestowed upon me,
and I confess to You my sin.
So forgive me, for nobody can forgive
sins except You.

Remember: It was narrated from Abu Musa that the Prophet said: "Allāh holds out His Hand at night to accept the repentance of those who have sinned during the day, and He holds out His Hand by day to accept the repentance of those who have sinned at night – until the sun rises from its place of setting."

[*Sahih Muslim*, Vol. 7, Remembrance, Supplication, Repentance and Praying for Forgiveness, Chapter 10, Hadith No. (6989) 31 – (2759)]

THE REWARD

BE PLEASED by the Best إِنْ شَاءَ اللَّهُ.

THE EVIDENCE

Thawban ؓ said: "The Messenger of Allah ﷺ said:
'Whoever says when he reaches the evening: "I am pleased with Allah as (my) Lord, with Islam as (my) religion, and with Muhammad as (my) Prophet (*Raditu Billahi Rabban Wabil-Islami Dinan Wa Bi-Muhammadin Nabiyan*)" it is a duty upon Allah to please him.'"

[*Jami' at-Tirmidhi*, Vol. 6, The Book of Supplications, Chapter 13, Hadith No. 3389]

THE WORDS

رَضِيتُ بِاللهِ رَبّاً

وَبِالْإِسْلَامِ دِيناً

وَبِمُحَمَّدٍ نَبِيّاً

Raḍītu billāhi rabban,
Wa bi-l-Islāmi dīnan,
Wa bi-Muḥammadin nabiyyan

I am pleased with Allāh as Lord, and
with Islam as Dīn and with Muḥammad
as Prophet.

Remember: Abu Sa'eed Al-Khudri ﷺ
narrated that the Messenger of Allah ﷺ
said: "Indeed, Allāh will say to the people
of Paradise: 'O people of Paradise!' They
will say: 'We respond to You, O our Lord,
and we are at Your service.' Then He will

63

say: 'Are you pleased?' They will say: 'Why should we not be pleased when You have given us what You have not given anyone from Your creation.' So He will say: 'I shall give you what is greater than that.' They will say: 'And what is greater than that?' He will say: 'I shall cover you in My Pleasure and I shall not become angry with you ever.'"

[*Jami' at-Tirmidhi*, Vol. 4, The Description of Paradise, Chapter 18, Hadith No. 2555]

THE REWARDS

B E FORGIVEN for what you do in the day. Be forgiven for what you do in the night إِنْ شَاءَ اللّٰهُ.

THE EVIDENCE

Anas ؓ narrated that the Messenger of Allah ﷺ said: "Whoever says in the morning: 'O Allah we have reached morning, calling You to witness, and calling the carriers of Your Throne to witness, and Your angels, and all of Your creation, that You are Allah, none has the right to be worshipped but You, Alone, without partner, and that Muhammad is Your slave and Your Messenger, (*Allahumma Asbahna Nush-hiduka Wa Nush-hidu Hamalata 'Arshika Wa Mala'ikataka Wa Jami'a Khalqika Bi-Annaka*

Allah, La Ilaha Illa Anta Wahdaka La Sharika Laka Wa Anna Muhammadan 'Abduka Wa Rasuluka)' Allah will forgive him for whatever he does that day, and if he says it in the evening, Allah will forgive him for whatever sin he commits that night."

[*Jami' at-Tirmidhi*, Vol. 6, The Book of Supplications, Chapter (...), Hadith No. 3501]

THE WORDS

اَللَّهُمَّ أَصْبَحْنَا نُشْهِدُكَ وَنُشْهِدُ حَمَلَةَ
عَرْشِكَ وَمَلَائِكَتَكَ وَجَمِيعَ خَلْقِكَ بِأَنَّكَ
اللّهُ لَا إِلَهَ إِلَّا أَنْتَ وَحَدَكَ لَا شَرِيكَ لَكَ
وَأَنَّ مُحَمَّداً عَبْدُكَ وَرَسُولِكَ

*Allāhumma aṣbaḥnā nush-hiduka
wa nush-hidu ḥamalata 'arshika wa
malā'ikataka wa jamī'a khalqika
bi-annaka-llāh, la ilāha illā Anta waḥdaka*

*lā sharīka laka, wa anna Muḥammadan
'abduka wa rasūluka*

O Allāh we have reached morning,
calling You to witness, and calling the
carriers of Your Throne to witness, and
Your angels, and all Your creation, that
You are Allāh, none has the right to
be worshipped but You, Alone without
partner, and that Muḥammad is Your
slave and Your Messenger

Remember: O Allāh! You are the Most
Merciful and the Most Patient. Instil
within us the wisdom, strength and
willpower to avoid committing sinful
acts and thus taking advantage of Your
infinite kindness. When we fall into error,
knowingly and unknowingly (despite our
efforts), forgive us O Allah and love us
always. *Āmīn.*

OTHER GEMS

THE REWARDS

EARN ONE million good deeds. Cancel one million bad deeds. Raise yourself one million levels إِنْ شَاءَ اللَّهُ.

THE EVIDENCE

Salim bin 'Abdullah bin 'Umar narrates from his father, from his grandfather, that the Messenger of Allah ﷺ said: "Whoever enters the marketplace and says: 'There is none worthy of worship except Allah, Alone, without partner, to Him belongs the dominion, and to Him is all the praise, He gives life and causes death, He is Living and does not die, in His Hand is the good, and He has power over all things, (*La Ilaha Illallah, Wahdahu La Sharika Lahu, Lahul-Mulku Wa Lahul-Hamdu, Yuhiyu Wa Yumitu, Wa Huwa Hayyun La Yamutu, Biyadihil-Khairu, Wa*

Huwa 'Ala Kulli Shai'in Qadir)' Allah shall record a million good deeds for him, wipe a million evil deeds away from him, and raise a million ranks for him."

[*Jami' at-Tirmidhi*, Vol. 6, The Book of Supplications, Chapter 36, Hadith No. 3428]

THE WORDS

لَاۤ إِلَهَ إِلَّا اللّٰهُ وَحْدَهُ لَا شَرِيكَ لَهُ،
لَهُ الْمُلْكُ وَلَهُ الْحَمْدُ،

يُحِيِي وَيُمِيتُ وَهُوَ حَيٌّ لَا يَمُوتُ،
بِيَدِهِ الْخَيْرُ، وَهُوَ عَلَى كُلِّ شَيْءٍ قَدِيرٌ

Lā ilāha illa-llāhu waḥdahu lā sharīka lah,
lahu-l-mulku wa lahu-l-ḥamd,
yuḥyī wa yumītu wa huwa ḥayyun lā yamūt,
bi yadihi-l-khayr,
wa huwa 'alā kulli shay'in qadīr

There is no god but Allāh alone without partner, to Him belongs dominion and praise, He causes life and death and He is the Living Who does not die. In His Hand is all good, and He is able to do all things.

Remember: This phenomenal *duʿā* gives a new meaning to collecting reward points when you go shopping! It also serves to remind us that although material objects may bring temporary pleasure in this life, our ultimate pleasure lies in ensuring that we have invested prudently for the eternal Afterlife إِنْ شَاءَ اللَّهُ.

THE REWARD

BE FORGIVEN for engaging in useless talk in a gathering إِنْ شَاءَ اللّٰهُ.

THE EVIDENCE

Abu Hurairah ﷺ narrated that the Messenger of Allah ﷺ said:

"Whoever sits in a sitting and engages in much empty, meaningless speech and then says before getting up from that sitting of his: 'Glory is to You, O Allah, and praise, I bear witness there is none worthy of worship except You, I seek Your forgiveness, and I repent to You, (*Subhanaka Allahumma Wa Bihamdika Wa Ashhadu An La Ilaha Illa Anta, Astaghfiruka Wa Atubu Ilaik*)' whatever occurred in that sitting would be forgiven to him."

[*Jami' at-Tirmidhi*, Vol. 6, The Book of Supplications, Chapter 38, Hadith No. 3433]

THE WORDS

سُبْحَانَكَ اللّٰهُمَّ وَبِحَمْدِكَ

أَشْهَدُ أَن لَّآ إِلٰهَ إِلَّآ أَنْتَ

أَسْتَغْفِرُكَ وَأَتُوبُ إِلَيْكَ

*Subhānak-Allāhumma wa bi ḥamdik,
ash-hadu al-lā ilāha illā ant,
astaghfiruka wa atūbu ilayk*

Glorious are You, O Allāh
and with Your Praise!
I witness that there is no god but You,
I seek Your forgiveness and I turn to
You (in repentance).

Remember: Abu Sa'eed Al-Khudri
narrated (that the Prophet) said:

"When the son of Adam wakes up in the morning, all of his body parts bow to the tongue and say: 'Fear Allah regarding us, we are only part of you. If you are straight we are straight, and if you are crooked we are crooked.'"

[*Jami' at-Tirmidhi*, Vol. 4, Chapters on *Zuhd*, Chapter 60, Hadith No. 2407]

THE REWARD

HAVE EIGHT gates of heaven open for you and enter through the gate of your choice إِنْ شَاءَ اللَّهُ.

THE EVIDENCE

It was narrated that 'Uqbah bin 'Amir ﷺ said: "We were charged with taking care of the camels. When my turn came, I brought them back in the evening and found the Messenger of Allah ﷺ standing up, addressing the people. I caught up with him when he was saying: 'There is no Muslim who performs *Wudu'* and does it well, then stands and prays two *Rak'ah* in which his heart is focused as he faces the *Qiblah*, but Paradise will be due to him.' I said: 'How good this (is)!' Someone who was in front of me said: 'What came before it was even better.' I looked and saw that it was 'Umar. He said: 'I see that you have just come; he said: "There is no one among you who performs *Wudu'* and does it completely – or he said *Fayusbighu* – then says: '*Ash-hadu An-la ilaha illallah, Wa Anna Muhammadan 'Abduhu Wa Rasuluh* (I bear witness that none has the right to be worshipped but Allah and that Muhammad is His slave and Messenger),' but the eight gates of Paradise will be opened to him, and he will enter through whichever one he wishes."

[*Sahih Muslim*, Vol. 1, The Book of Purification, Chapter 6, Hadith No. (553) 17 – (234)]

THE WORDS

أَشْهَدُ أَن لَّا إِلَهَ إِلَّا اللَّهُ،

وَأَنَّ مُحَمَّداً عَبْدُهُ وَرَسُولُهُ

Ashhadu al-lā ilāha illa-llāh,
wa anna Muḥammadan 'abduhu warasūluh

I bear witness that
there is no god but Allāh
and that Muḥammad
is His slave and Messenger.

Remember: *(Their greeting will be):*
"Enter ye here in Peace and Security."
And We shall remove from their hearts
any lurking sense of injury: (They will be)
brothers (joyfully) facing each other on
thrones (of dignity). There no sense of fatigue
shall touch them, nor shall they (ever) be
asked to leave.

[Holy Qur'ān, Sūrat al-Ḥijr 15:46-48]

THE REWARDS

HAVE TEN good deeds written for you. Have ten evil deeds wiped away from you. Be raised ten degrees. Be in security all that day from every disliked thing. Be protected from the *shayṭān*. Ensure no sin can destroy you (except *shirk*) إِنْ شَاءَ اللَّه.

THE EVIDENCE

Abu Dharr ؓ narrated that the Messenger of Allah ﷺ said: "Whoever says at the end of every *Fajr* prayer, while his feet are still folded, before speaking: 'None has the right to be worshipped but Allah, Alone without partner, to Him belongs all that exists, and to Him is the praise, He gives life and causes death, and He is powerful over all things, (*La Ilaha Illallah, Wahdahu La Sharika Lahu, Lahul-Mulku Wa Lahul-Hamdu, Yuhyi Wa Yumitu, Wa Huwa 'Ala Kulli Shai'in Qadir*)' ten times, then ten good deeds shall be written for him, ten evil deeds shall be wiped away from him, ten degrees shall be raised up for him, and he shall be in security all that day from every disliked thing, and he shall be in protection from *Shaitan*, and no sin will meet him or destroy him that day, except for associating partners with Allah."

[*Jami' at-Tirmidhi*, Vol. 6, The Book of Supplications, Chapter 62, Hadith No. 3474]

The Words

لَاۤ إِلَهَ إِلَّا اللَّهُ وَحْدَهُ لَا شَرِيكَ لَهُ،

لَهُ الْمُلْكُ وَلَهُ الْحَمْدُ،

يُحْيِي وَيُمِيتُ،

وَهُوَ عَلَى كُلِّ شَيْءٍ قَدِيرٌ (١٠)

Lā ilāha illa-llāhu waḥdahu lā sharīka lah,
lahu-l-mulku wa lahu-l-ḥamd,
yuḥyī wa yumīt,
wa huwa ʿalā kulli shayʾin qadīr (x10)

There is no god but Allāh alone without
partner, to Him belongs the kingdom
and His is the Praise,
He gives life and causes death,
and He has power over all things (x10)

Remember: There are two actions that are normally light and easy to do but become extremely difficult to perform at *Fajr* time – opening our eyes and lifting our blankets! We should try remembering this *duʿā* to give ourselves yet another good reason to wake up for *Fajr ṣalāh* إِنْ شَاءَ اللَّهُ.

EASY
SUNNAH
DEEDS

THE MESSENGER of Allah said:
"That indeed whoever revives
a *Sunnah* from my *Sunnah* which
has died after me, then for him is a
reward similar to whoever acts upon
it without diminishing anything from
their rewards."

[*Jami' at-Tirmidhi*, Vol. 5, The Chapters on Knowledge, Chapter 16, Hadith No. 2677]

It was narrated from 'Abdullah bin 'Amr, that a man asked the Messenger of Allah: "What part of Islam is best?" He said: "Offering food, and saying *Salam* to those whom you know, and those whom you do not know."

[*Sunan Abu Dawud*, Vol. 5, The Book of Etiquette, Chapter 130, 131, Hadith No. 5194]

It was narrated that Abu Umamah ﷺ said: "The Messenger of Allah ﷺ said: 'The one who is closest of people to Allah, the Most High, is the one who initiates the greeting of *Salam*.'"

[*Sunan Abu Dawud*, Vol. 5, The Book of Etiquette, Chapter 132, 133, Hadith No. 5197]

It was narrated that Abu Dharr ﷺ said: "The Prophet ﷺ said to me: 'Do not regard any act of kindness as insignificant, even meeting your brother with a cheerful countenance.'"

[*Sahih Muslim*, Vol. 6, The Book of *Al-Birr*, Nurturing Ties and Manners, Chapter 43, Hadith No. (6690) 144 – (2626)]

It was narrated that Abu Hurairah ﷺ said: "The Messenger of Allah ﷺ said: 'By the One in Whose Hand is my soul, you will not enter Paradise until you believe, and you will not believe until you love one another. Shall I not tell you of something which, if you do it, you will love one another? Spread *Salam* among yourselves.'"

[*Sunan Abu Dawud*, Vol. 5, The Book of Etiquette, Chapter 130, 131, Hadith No. 5193]

It was narrated that 'Imran bin Husain ﷺ said: "A man came to the Prophet ﷺ and said: '*As-Salamu 'alaikum* (peace be upon you)' and he returned the greeting, then he sat down. The Prophet ﷺ said: '*Ten*.' Another man came, and said: '*As-Salamu 'alaikum wa rahmatullah* (Peace be upon you and the mercy of Allah),' and he returned the greeting, then he sat down. The Prophet ﷺ said: '*Twenty*.' Another man came and said: '*As-Salamu 'alaikum wa rahmatullahi wa barakatuhu* (Peace be upon you and the mercy of Allah and His blessings),' and he returned the greeting, then he sat down. The Prophet ﷺ said: '*Thirty*.'"

[*Sunan Abu Dawud*, Vol. 5, The Book of Etiquette, Chapter 131, 132, Hadith No. 5195]

Al-Bara' bin 'Azib ؓ narrated that the Messenger of Allah ﷺ said:

"No two Muslims meet each other and shake hands, except that Allah forgives them before they part."

[*Jami' at-Tirmidhi*, Vol. 5, The Chapters on Seeking Permission, Chapter 31, Hadith No. 2727]

It was narrated from Anas bin Malik ﷺ that a man was with the Prophet ﷺ, when another man passed by, and he said: "O Messenger of Allah, I love this man." The Prophet ﷺ said to him: "Have you told him?" He said: "No." He said: "Tell him." So he caught up with him and said: "I love you for the sake of Allah." He said: "May the One for Whose sake you love me, also love you."

[*Sunan Abu Dawud*, Vol. 5, The Book of Etiquette, Chapter 112, 113, Hadith No. 5125]

Abu Hurairah ﷺ narrated that the Messenger of Allah ﷺ saw a man laying on his stomach so he said:

"Indeed such a laying is not loved by Allah."

[*Jami' at-Tirmidhi*, Vol. 5, The Chapters on Manners, Chapter 21, Hadith No. 2768]

Anas bin Malik ﷺ said: "(The Messenger of Allah ﷺ) fixed the time for us for paring the moustache, trimming the fingernails, shaving the pubic hairs and plucking the underarm hairs – that we not leave it for more than forty days."

[*Jami' At-Tirmidhi*, Vol. 5, The Chapters on Manners, Chapter 15, Hadith No. 2759]

It was narrated from Ibn 'Umar that the Prophet ﷺ said: "Trim the moustache and let the beard grow."

[*Sahih Muslim*, Vol. 1, The Book of Purification, Chapter 16, Hadith No. (600) 52 - (259)]

Narrated 'Aishah : The Prophet used to like starting from the right in performing ablution, combing his hair and putting on his shoes.

[*Sahih al-Bukhari*, Vol. 7, The Book of Dress, Chapter 38, Hadith No. 5854]

Narrated Abu Hurairah ﷺ: Allah's Messenger ﷺ said, "If you want to put on your shoes, put on the right shoe first; and if you want to take them off, take off the left one first. Let the right shoe be the first to be put on and the last to be taken off."

[*Sahih al-Bukhari*, Vol. 7, The Book of Dress, Chapter 40, Hadith No. 5856]

Samurah bin Jundab ☙ said: "The Messenger of Allah ☙ said: 'Wear white, for indeed it is very pure and cleaner, and shroud your dead in it.'"

[*Jami' at-Tirmidhi*, Vol.5, The Chapters on Manners, Chapter 46, Hadith No. 2810]

'Aishah ﷺ said: "Whoever narrated to you that the Prophet ﷺ would urinate while standing; then don't believe him. He would not urinate except while squatting."

[*Jami' at-Tirmidhi*, Vol. 1, The Chapters on Purification, Chapter 8, Hadith No. 12]

Narrated Abu Qatada ﷺ: The Prophet ﷺ said,

"Whenever anyone of you urinates, he should neither hold his penis with his right hand nor clean his private parts with his right hand."

[*Sahih al-Bukhari*, Vol. 1, The Book of *Wudu'*, Chapter 19, Hadith No. 154]

Abu Sa'eed 🙵 narrated that he heard the Messenger of Allah 🙵 say:

"Let not two people who go out to the toilet (*Gha'it*) to relieve themselves (such that) their private parts are uncovered, talking to one another. Verily Allah, the Mighty and Sublime, hates that."

[*Sunan Abu Dawud*, Vol. 1, The Book of Purification, Chapter 7, Hadith No. 15]

Narrated Abu Ayyub Al-Ansari ☺: Allah's Messenger ☺ said, "If anyone of you goes to an open space for answering the call of nature he should neither face nor turn his back towards the *Qiblah*; he should either face the east or the west."

[*Sahih al-Bukhari*, Vol. 1, The Book of *Wudu'*, Chapter 11, Hadith No. 144]

Narrated 'Umar bin Abi Salama : I was a boy under the care of Allah's Messenger  and my hand used to go around the dish while eating. So Allah's Messenger  said to me, "O Boy! Mention the Name of Allah and eat with your right hand, and eat of the dish what is nearer to you." Since then I have applied those instructions while eating.

[*Sahih al-Bukhari*, Vol. 7, The Book of Foods (Meals), Chapter 2, Hadith No. 5376]

It was narrated that Abu Hurairah ﷺ said: "The Messenger of Allah ﷺ never criticised any food. If he liked something he would eat it, and if he disliked it he would leave it."

[*Sahih Muslim*, Vol. 5, The Book of Drinks, Chapter 35, Hadith No. (5380) 187 – (2064)]

It was narrated from Ibn Ka'b bin Malik that his father ﷺ said: "The Messenger of Allah ﷺ used to eat with three fingers, and lick his hand before wiping it."

[*Sahih Muslim*, Vol. 5, The Book of Drinks, Chapter 18, Hadith No. (5297) (...)]

It was narrated that Anas bin Malik ﷺ said: "The Messenger of Allah ﷺ said: 'Allah is pleased with a person who eats some food and then praises Him for it, or who drinks some drink and then praises Him for it.'"

[*Sahih Muslim*, Vol. 7, Remembrance, Supplication, Repentance and Praying for Forgiveness, Chapter 24, Hadith No. (6932) 89 – (2734)]

It was narrated from Abu Bakr bin 'Ubaidullah bin 'Abdullah bin 'Umar, from his grandfather Ibn 'Umar ﷺ, that the Messenger of Allah ﷺ said: "When one of you eats, let him eat with his right hand, and when he drinks, let him drink with his right hand, for the *Shaitan* eats with his left hand and drinks with his left hand."

[*Sahih Muslim*, Vol. 5, The Book of Drinks, Chapter 13, Hadith No. 5265]

It was narrated that Jabir ﷺ said: "The Messenger of Allah ﷺ said: 'If one of you drops a morsel, let him pick it up and remove any dirt on it, then let him eat it, and not leave it for the *Shaitan*. And he should not wipe his hand with the cloth until he has licked his fingers, for he does not know in which part of the food the blessing is.'"

[*Sahih Muslim*, Vol. 5, The Book of Drinks, Chapter 18, Hadith No. (5301) 134 – (...)]

Abu Qatadah narrated that the Prophet said: "The one providing water for people is the last of them to drink."

[*Jami' at-Tirmidhi*, Vol. 3, The Chapters on Drinks, Chapter 20, Hadith No. 1894]

It was narrated that Anas ﷺ said: "The Messenger of Allah ﷺ used to breathe three times when drinking, and he would say: 'It is more thirst-quenching, healthier and more wholesome.'"

[*Sahih Muslim*, Vol. 5, The Book of Drinks, Chapter 16, Hadith No. (5287) 123 – (...)]

It was narrated that Abu Sa'eed Al-Khudri said: "The Messenger of Allah forbade drinking from the cracked place on a cup, and blowing into a drink."

[*Sunan Abu Dawud*, Vol. 4, The Book of Drinks, Chapter 16, Hadith No. 3722]

It was narrated from 'Abdullah bin Abi Qatadah, from his father , that the Prophet ﷺ forbade breathing into the vessel.

[*Sahih Muslim*, Vol. 5, The Book of Drinks, Chapter 16, Hadith No. (5285) 121 – (267)]

Narrated Anas bin Malik ﷺ: Milk mixed with water was brought to Allah's Messenger ﷺ while a bedouin was on his right and Abu Bakr ﷺ was on his left. He drank (of it) and then gave (it) to the bedouin and said, "The right." "The right (first)."

[*Sahih al-Bukhari*, Vol. 7, The Book of Drinks, Chapter 18, Hadith No. 5619]

It was narrated from Anas that the Prophet forbade drinking whilst standing. Qatadah said: "We said: 'What about eating?' He said: 'That is worse, or more abhorrent.'"

[*Sahih Muslim*, Vol. 5, The Book of Drinks, Chapter 14, Hadith No. (5275) 113 – (...)]

It was narrated that Abu Ad-Darda' 🙏 said: "The Messenger of Allah 🙏 said: 'There is no Muslim who prays for his brother in his absence, but the angel says: And you will have something similar.'"

[*Sahih Muslim*, Vol. 7, Remembrance, Supplication, Repentance and Praying for Forgiveness, Chapter 23, Hadith No. (6927) 86 – (2732)]

It was narrated that Abu Hurairah ﷺ said: "The Messenger of Allah ﷺ said: 'Whoever removes a worldly hardship from a believer, Allah will remove one of the hardships of the Day of Resurrection from him. Whoever grants respite to (a debtor) who is in difficulty, Allah will grant him relief in this world and in the Hereafter. Whoever conceals (the fault of) a Muslim in this world, Allah will conceal him (his faults) in this world and in the Hereafter. Allah will help a person so long as he is helping his brother. Whoever follows a path seeking knowledge, Allah will make a path to Paradise easy for him. No people gather in one of the houses of Allah, reciting the Book of Allah and studying it together, but tranquillity will descend upon them, mercy will overshadow them, the angels will surround them and Allah will mention them to those who are with Him. Whoever is slowed down by his deeds, his lineage will not help him to get ahead.'"

[*Sahih Muslim*, Vol. 7, Remembrance, Supplication, Repentance and Praying for Forgiveness, Chapter 11, Hadith No. (6853) 38 – (2966)]

It was narrated from Abu Hurairah ﷺ that the Prophet ﷺ said: "A man visited a brother of his in another town, and Allah sent an angel to wait for him on the road. When he came to him, he said, 'Where are you headed?' He said: 'I am headed to a brother of mine in this town.' He said: 'Have you done him any favour for which you hope to be recompensed?' He said: 'No, but I love him for the sake of Allah (the Mighty and Sublime).' He said: 'I am a messenger from Allah to you, to tell you that Allah loves you as you love him for His sake.'"

[*Sahih Muslim*, Vol. 6, The Book of *Al-Birr*, Nurturing Ties and Manners, Chapter 12, Hadith No. (6549) 38 – (2567)]

Anas ﷺ said: "When we were with the Messenger of Allah ﷺ it rained. The Messenger of Allah ﷺ lifted part of his garment so that the rain could fall on him. We said: 'O Messenger of Allah, why did you do that?' He said: 'Because it has just come from its Lord, the Mighty and Sublime.'"

[*Sahih Muslim*, Vol. 2, The Book of Prayer Seeking Rain (*Al-Istisqa'*), Chapter 2, Hadith No. (2083) 13 – (898)]

Narrated Jabir bin 'Abdullah ![image_ref](): Whenever we went up a place we would say "*Allahu Akbar* (i.e. Allah is the Most Great)", and whenever we went down a place we would say: "*Subhan Allah.*"

[*Sahih al-Bukhari*, Vol. 4, The Book of *Jihad* (Fighting for Allah's Cause), Chapter 132, Hadith No. 2993]

Narrated Abu Mas'ud Al-Ansari ﷺ: The Prophet ﷺ said, "When a Muslim spends something on his family intending to receive Allah's reward, it is regarded as *Sadaqa* (act of charity) for him."

[*Sahih al-Bukhari*, Vol. 7, The Book of Provision: (Outlay), Chapter 1, Hadith No. 5351]

Narrated Al-Aswad: I asked 'Aishah 🙵 what did the Prophet 🙵 use to do at home? She replied, "He used to keep himself busy serving his family and when it was time for the *Salat* (prayer), he would get up for *Salat* (prayer)."

[*Sahih al-Bukhari*, Vol. 8, The Book of *Al-Adab* (Good Manners), Chapter 40, Hadith No. 6039]

Narrated Abu Hurairah 🙐: The Prophet ﷺ said, "If anyone of you sneezes, he should say, '*Al-Hamdu-lillah*' (praise be to Allah), and his (Muslim) brother or companion should say to him '*Yar-hamukallah*' (may Allah bestow His Mercy on you). When the latter says, '*Yar-hamukallah*', the former should say '*Yah-dikumullah wa Yuslih balakum*' (may Allah give you guidance and improve your condition)."

[*Sahih al-Bukhari*, Vol. 8, The Book of *Al-Adab* (Good Manners), Chapter 126, Hadith No. 6224]

Narrated Abu Hurairah ﷺ: The Prophet ﷺ said,

"Allah likes sneezing and dislikes yawning, so if someone sneezes and then praises Allah, then it is obligatory on every Muslim who heard him, to say: May Allah be Merciful to you (*Yar-hamukallah*). But as regards yawning, it is from Satan, so one must try his best to stop it as much as possible; if one says '*Ha*' when yawning, Satan will laugh at him."

[*Sahih al-Bukhari*, Vol. 8, The Book of *Al-Adab* (Good Manners), Chapter 125, Hadith No. 6223]

It was narrated from Zuhair, from Suhail, from Ibn Abi Sa'eed Al-Khudri that his father said: "The Messenger of Allah said: 'When one of you yawns, let him cover his mouth, lest the *Shaitan* enter.'"

[*Sunan Abu Dawud*, Vol. 5, The Book of Etiquette, Chapter 89, Hadith No. 5026]

It was reported from Abu 'Abdur-Rahman, meaning Al-Hubuli, from 'Abdullah bin 'Amr ﷺ, that a man said: "O Messenger of Allah! The *Mu'adhdhins* have been favored over us!" So the Messenger of Allah ﷺ said: "Say as they say, then, when you finish, ask (what you wish), and you will be given it."

[*Sunan Abu Dawud*, Vol. 1, The Book of *Salat* (The Prayer), Chapter 36, Hadith No. 524]

POSTFACE

THIS LITTLE book contains many merciful blessings from our Lord and Creator, Allāh ﷻ, but there are two more blessings in my life that cannot be found within these pages – my beloved mother and my beloved father. The words that they taught, the hardships that they endured, and the sacrifices that they made meant that we never had to wander far from home to find the beautiful light of Islam; الْحَمْدُ لِلَّه. May Allāh ﷻ forgive them, ease their burdens and grant them *Jannat al-Firdaws*.

Āmīn.

N. J. Islam

A NOTE TO THE READER

THE ĀYĀT in the 'Remember' sections are English translations sourced from *The Meaning of the Holy Qur'ān* (see 'References') and have been included with the kind permission of the respected publisher.

There are slight differences between the text within the *aḥādīth* in 'The Evidence' and the content within 'The Words' section. This is due in the former case to our respecting the published editions, and in the latter case to our giving as exact a transliteration as possible for the benefit of the reader who has not learnt Arabic.

All *aḥādīth* present within this book have been sourced from *Ṣaḥīḥ Muslim, Jāmiʿ At-Tirmidhī, Sunan Abū Dāwūd,* and *Ṣaḥīḥ Al-Bukhārī* (see 'References') and have been included with the kind permission of the respected publisher.

The 'Remember' segments are an assortment of quotes and personal thoughts included by the compiler.

The texts in gold within the 'Easy Sunnah Deeds' highlight the 'quick wins' within each *hadith* إِنْ شَاءَ اللَّهُ.

Please feel free to add your own favourite *duʿās* to the blank pages at the back of your book!

REFERENCES

THE MEANING OF THE HOLY QUR'AN

English Translation by Abdullah Yusuf Ali, 11th edition (Beltsville, Maryland, amana publications, 2009)

SAHIH MUSLIM

Imam Abdul Hussain Muslim bin al-Hajjaj, Hafiz Abu Tahir Zubair 'Ali Za'i, Nasiruddin al-Khattab, Huda Khattab, Abu Khaliyl (2007) English Translation of *Sahih Muslim,* Volumes 1, 2, 5, 6 and 7 Darussalam

JAMI' AT-TIRMIDHI

Imam Hafiz Abu 'Eisa Mohammad Ibn 'Eisa At-Tirmidhi, Abu Khaliyl, Hafiz Abu Tahir Zubair 'Ali Za'i (2007) English Translation of *Jami' At-Tirmidhi,* Volumes 1, 3, 4, 5 and 6 Darussalam

SUNAN ABU DAWUD

Imam Hafiz Abu Dawud Sulaiman bin Ash'ath, Hafiz Abu Tahir Zubair 'Ali Za'i, Yasir Qadhi, Abu Khaliyl (2008) English Translation of *Sunan Abu Dawud,* Volumes 1, 2, 4 and 5 Darussalam

SAHIH AL-BUKHARI

Dr. Muhammad Mushin Khan (1997) The Translation of the Meanings of *Sahih Al-Bukhari.* Arabic-English, Volumes 1, 4, 7, 8 and 9, Darussalam Publishers and Distributors

YOUR OWN DU'AS

Editor's Note

Ahadith on:
Page 9 and 103 are *Da'if*
Page 10 is *Da'if/Hasan Gharib Sahih**
Page 13 (Hadith No. 2898) is *Da'if*
Page 27 and 72 are *Da'if/Gharib**
Page 47 and 93 is *Da'if/Hasan Gharib**
Page 87 is *Da'if/Hasan**

*According to Abu 'Eisa